GRAVESEND

IN OLD PHOTOGRAPHS

GRAVESEND
IN OLD PHOTOGRAPHS

COLLECTED BY

ROBERT H. HISCOCK

ALAN SUTTON
1988

Alan Sutton Publishing Limited
Brunswick Road · Gloucester

First published 1988

British Library Cataloguing in Publication Data

Gravesend in old photographs.
1. Gravesend, history
I. Hiscock, Robert H.
942.2'315

ISBN 0-86299-514-0

FRONT COVER St Andrews Church (built in 1871 and designed by the architect G.E. Street)
and Bawley Bay c.1872. Thames Terrace and Sussex Place to the left. On the right is R.V.
Maynell's ship-repairing yard with St George's steeple. St Andrews closed in 1971 and is
now an arts centre (Gravesend Library)

Typesetting and origination by
Alan Sutton Publishing Limited.
Printed in Great Britain
by WBC Print Limited.

CONTENTS

INTRODUCTION AND ACKNOWLEDGEMENTS

There are Histories of Gravesend by R. Pocock 1797, R.P. Cruden 1843, F.A. Mansfield 1922, A.J. Philips 1954, J. Benson and R.H. Hiscock 1976 and S. Harker (which covers Gravesham) 1979 to which the reader is referred for the long and interesting history of the town going back to the Norman Conquest and beyond; both Gravesend and Milton being of Saxon origin. This, however, is a book illustrating the changing scene in Gravesend over the last hundred years or so and a few of the people who have lived and worked in the town.

The old Borough which was incorporated in 1562 consisted of the ancient parishes of Gravesend and Milton-next-Gravesend, the boundary between the two running down the present High Street, Windmill Street and Singlewell Road, the southern boundary being reached at Gypsy Corner and Claphall. In 1935 the Borough was extended to take in Denton and Chalk to the east and Singlewell and Watling Street to the south. In 1974 the new Authority of Gravesham (the Domesday form of the name) added the Urban District of Northfleet to the west as well as a number of rural parishes to the east and south.

This photographic survey is confined to the area of the 1935 Borough (but excepting Chalk) and to Rosherville Gardens which, although just over the Northfleet boundary, were always associated with Gravesend. The population of Gravesend in 1881 was 22,000; in 1981, 53,000 (this included the area added in 1935).

I have divided this book into six sections: 1. The Waterside; 2. The Main Road, known as Rochester Road, Milton Road, King Street (which originally led into the High Street), New Road (a completely new straight road to Northfleet cut in 1801 by the Turnpike Commissioners) and Overcliffe (formerly part of New Road);

3. The Old Road (which prior to 1801 was the Turnpike London–Dover road) from its junction with Rochester Road at the Lion Garage to the Northfleet boundary; 4. Watling Street, now the motorised A2, but until 1923 (when it became the Gravesend bypass) a narrow but straight country lane of Roman or earlier origin running about two miles to the south of the river. In each case the views start at the east and work west and include some views on each side. In Section 5 I have included views of the old parish churches of Gravesend and Milton, as well as Ifield, an isolated church just over the 1935 boundary but which serves Singlewell. In addition I have included the three Victorian churches, all of which have been pulled down (but in the case of Christ Church erected on another site), and the Roman Catholic Church of St John, formerly an Anglican Proprietory Chapel. Local transport has played a large part in the expansion of the town during the last hundred years and Section 6 deals with this.

This collection of photographs is the result of a joint effort by the Gravesend Public Library and the Gravesend Historical Society, while many come from Cyril Ford and Eric Green's vast collection and those of Douglas Grierson, Ernest Tilley and Tony Larkin, without whose help and co-operation this volume would not have been possible: I am deeply grateful to them. The selection however is entirely my own and shows people and views which interest me, but which I think can be taken as representative and I hope will interest others. I have deliberately not dealt with either of the Wars or the great changes in the town which have taken place since 1950 with the rebuilding of much of the central area.

A number of the earlier views are from an album belonging to Brian Hayes but which came to me through the Ford-Green collection. They appear to be by F.S. Gould, a well-known local and marine photographer, many of whose plates are now in the Gravesend Library and National Maritime Museum. In many cases those used here are different from the Library collection and have not been published before, and I am very appreciative of Mr Hayes' permission to use them.

I hope all the acknowledgements are correct. Some views are of course in a number of collections and I have merely acknowledged the one from which I borrowed the photograph. My apologies to anyone whose consent I ought to have obtained but have not. It is difficult to trace the origin of some pictures. Those which are not acknowledged come from my own collection and I thank all of those who in the past have given me local photographs and material. I hope by publishing them many more will be able to enjoy some of the wealth of local illustrations which are available in this area to show the changing scene in Gravesend over the last hundred years.

My thanks are also due to Mrs D. Roots, my secretary, for typing the manuscript.

CANAL BASIN c.1880. To the right, the gasworks and the crane used for unloading its coal. Across the bridge lay Huggins & Co. soapworks, Geo. Butchard Milton ironworks (later Priestleys), E. & H. Sandfords engineering works and Hayward & Walter fish manure merchants (the area was noted for its odours). (B. Hayes, from the Ford-Green Collection.)

CANAL BASIN 1910. Lock keepers' cottages, Sandfords is to the right, and beyond these a coal hulk can be seen in the river complete with cranes for unloading coal into barges and lighters for the gas and electricity works.

THE BOAT HOUSE c.1900, with an upturned boat for a roof, is thought to have been the original of Peggotty's boat house in Dickens' *David Copperfield*. It was built c.1815 and demolished in 1942.

THE CANAL Denton Swing Bridge c.1905. The Thames and Medway Canal cut in 1824 remained open to Higham until 1935.

THE LOCK KEEPERS' COTTAGES, Canal Basin, shortly before demolition in 1974.

25149 Gravesend. The Canal Lock.

BARGES WAITING TO ENTER THE CANAL BASIN, c.1901, before the Sailing Club clubhouse was built and the promenade completed.

THE PROMENADE. c.1900, constructed when a schooner called *The Spring* ran ashore in 1886 laden with cement sacks which solidified and can be seen here. They remained visible until 1987 when the wall was rebuilt. In the distance is the Commercial Hotel (demolished c.1930) where Dickens is said to have stayed. Beyond it stood the Sailors' Home which became the Sea School in 1918 and was demolished in 1975. (Gravesend Library.)

CHILDREN ON PROMENADE BEACH c.1890. (B. Hayes, from the Ford-Green Collection.)

RIVERSIDE PROMENADE, GRAVESEND   L 692

THE PROMENADE c.1930 with holiday crowds.

UNVEILING OF THE STATUE OF GENERAL C. GORDON, 4 October 1893. The grounds and the statue were presented by George Matthews Arnold (p. 66) who can be seen wearing the mayoral chain. In the front row from the left are W.J. King, Borough Treasurer; G. Penman, Borough Coroner; next but one is W.T. Archer, builder; then S. Penny, Trinity House pilot; J. Rose, tailor (High Street); H.H. Stephenson and, behind him, W.H. Russell, stockbroker. The bearded figure is W. Wilks, stonemason. (For the Aldermen see p. 86). (Ford-Green Collection.)

GORDON GARDENS c. 1905.

FORT HOUSE from the rear c.1903. This was the house occupied from 1866–71 by General Gordon when he was Commanding Officer of the Royal Engineers, in charge of refurbishing the river defences. It had been moved about 200 yards on rollers when the New Tavern Fort was built in 1779.

FORT HOUSE front, or west, side. At one time the residence of the Town Clerk, W.A. Coombes, and later a school when there was no resident Governor. It became the Food Office in 1939 and was destroyed on 29 November 1944 by a V2.

FORT GARDENS. The Fort was acquired by the Corporation in 1932, laid out as public gardens and opened on 8 June by the Earl of Darnley as part of the Mayoral Tercentenary Celebrations. Fort House acquired 'Tudorbethan' beams and a bandstand was built.

THE GRAVESEND SWIMMING CLUB, NEW BRIDGE c.1909. The Thames was still clean enough for bathing and a race across the river was the great event of the season.

THE TEMPORARY TERRACE PIER c. 1835, from a print. The town pier, opened in 1834, can also be seen. In between the piers are Becketts Brewery, The Old Falcon and the Three Daws, with St George's Tower to the left.

THE TERRACE PIER 1895, built in 1842 by J.B. Redman. It was purchased from the Receiver in 1893 by the Trinity House Pilots, whose HQ it is, and it was restored by Messrs E.A. & H. Sandford in 1894. This shows the great frost when the Thames was frozen.

BAWLEY BOATS. Nets drying after shrimping c.1890.

SHRIMPS being caught and boiled off Leigh-on-Sea. (Pickering, Ford-Green Collection.)

Old Falcon Hotel, Gravesend

RIVERSIDE C.1905, showing The Old Falcon Hotel, the Amsterdam, Geo. Wood & Sons Brewery (they took over from Becketts in 1858 and sold to Russells in 1912), St Andrews built in 1870 and the Terrace Pier. (Tilley Collection.)

MUDLARKING. Boys digging in the mud for pennies thrown down by visitors, alongside The New Falcon, built in 1882 and demolished in 1954. The glazed building on the roof was at one time used as a studio by Charles Wylie, the marine artist. (Ford-Green Collection.)

'THE YOUNG STRIKER.' Harpum's forge, Queen Street. W.G. Harpum and his three sons. (E. Reader, from the Ford-Green Collection.)

THE AMSTERDAM, East Street frontage c.1890. At one time the Corporation 'breakfast' after Mayor-making was held here. George Wood's house and brewery were next door. The end wall of The Clarendon can be seen at the end of 'The Cut'.

HIGH STREET c.1900. G. & W. Morton (later Dicks) shoe shop to the left with its rival, Henry Moore (site of the first Woolworths), a little further along the street. Elkington (tailors) can be seen on the right-hand side.

PIGS AWAITING SLAUGHTER at Bloomfields slaughterhouse between the High Street and Queen Street. In 1905 there were 14 slaughterhouses in the town, seven built of wood and seven of brick.

HIGH STREET c.1905. On the right are the London Provincial Bank (later Barclays) and the classical front of the old Town Hall (added in 1834, A.H. Wilds being the architect and W.M. Wood the builder). To the left is The Jubilee, later part of Woolworths, and The Maypole.

INTERIOR, TOWN HALL, 1949, on the occasion of the Gravesend Historical Society's Silver Jubilee Soirée. Back row: -?-, J.S. Kean, A.J. Philip, Revd A.A. Burrows, J.T. Grant, R.H. Hiscock, -?-, Mayor Cllr. E.E. Osborne, Ongly-Miller (HM Art School), Canon H.J. Powell, Rector of Milton. Among those in front are A. King, Mrs Whitfield, Misses M. & A. Haill, Miss T. Jackson, J. Benson, D. Spain, L. Leach and Mrs K.P. Hiscock. (Gravesend Historical Society Collection.)

HIGH STREET c.1950. The weather-boarded shops on the left were built c.1730 after the 1727 fire and were demolished c.1960. (Kent Messenger.)

TOWN PIER SQUARE c.1900. Three Daws to the right. Hoppers with their 'impedimenta' (about which complaints were made in the local paper from time to time). They came down from London by the London Tilbury and Southend Railway whose fares at $\frac{1}{2}d$. per mile undercut the SER. (Ford-Green Collection.)

TOWN PIER SQUARE flooded c.1905. As early as 1905 a committee was set up to build a Thames barrier to prevent flooding, which occurred regularly in the lower parts of the town. The pier was bought by the LT & SR in 1886 and became its Gravesend station. Note the cast iron roof on the urinal to the left. (Larkin Collection)

FERRY CREWS Including Kendrick (father and son) on *The Earl of Essex* c.1900. The ferries were coaled by men carrying wicker baskets on their backs, hence the straw hat. This system continued until the end of the steam era in 1961. (Ford-Green Collection.)

EARL OF ESSEX LT & SR paddle ferry leaving Town Pier. (Grierson Collection)

TILBURY DOCKS, Tidal Basin 1, opened in 1886, had a great impact on Gravesend as many of the workers lived there as well as personnel who worked on the ships.

RMS *ORMUZ*, 6387 tons, the first Orient Pacific to come to Tilbury (on 15 January 1887) when the line moved from Liverpool. At that time it was the largest liner ever to come up the Thames.

CAPTAIN AND OFFICERS, RMS *OROYA* 1897, a sister ship to the *Ormuz* although somewhat smaller (6297 tons). On the right is Robert Turnbull, my maternal grandfather, later Commodore Engineer of the Line, who was also Chief Engineer on the *Ormuz*.

SHIPPING IN THE RIVER c.1912. To the left is an Orient ship, and to the right the ferry *Gertrude*, built in 1906 at Robertson's yard, as a sister to the *Edith*, 1911, with a wide open foredeck to carry cattle and vehicles. It was sold in 1931 to the Medway Steam Packet Co. and re-named *Rochester Queen*. (Larkin Collection.)

SUTHERLAND'S ANCHOR-RETRIEVING BOATS with the PLA diver c.1905. The anchors were either refurbished or sold for scrap. (Ford-Green Collection.)

THE SOUTH SIDE OF WEST STREET flooded in 1921, and later demolished c.1925. Suttie's Alley is to the left. (Ford-Green Collection.)

HOLE IN THE WALL ALLEY c.1890, leading from High Street to Princes Street, with the south end of Suttie's Alley on the right. The men are 'picking rags' to sell for a few coppers for paper-making. (Pickering, Ford-Green Collection.)

PASSENGERS COURT c.1890. One of the numerous courts and alleys between Church Street and West Street which was demolished c.1925. The area was hosed down weekly with disinfectant by the Council in the nineteenth and early twentieth centuries to keep diseases such as cholera at bay.

CHURCH STREET corner of Chapel Lane c.1920. The second-hand shop on the corner was the Gravesend post office in the 1820s and residence of Thomas Killick, post master and organist at St George's. The brick building to the left was the hop store for Russells Brewery.

WESTSIDE PLACE c.1930. This was to the south of Church Street and on the west side of St George's churchyard, built c.1830 and demolished in 1964. (J.S. Kean.)

CHURCH MISSION CHILDREN c.1880, the 'ragamuffins' and 'guttersnipes' whom the Ragged School and various church missions tried to educate and look after. (Gravesend Library.)

THE GORDON MISSION in 1955 just before demolition. This was the Ragged School, built in 1862 by W. Gould, successor to an earlier building and re-named in 1914. It provided free education when the church schools charged 2*d*. or 3*d*. per week. It also provided a soup kitchen, crèche (from 1914) and other welfare activities. General Gordon worked here. The mission moved to Valley Drive in 1932. (Gravesend Library.)

RAGGED SCHOOL OUTING c.1900. Horse vehicles assembled in Harmer Street, (built in 1834). (Ford-Green Collection.)

THE LAST REMNANT OF EDWARD III's ROYAL MANOR HOUSE, which came to light in 1949 immediately to the north of the Ragged School (the north wall of which can be seen to the left), being examined by members of the Gravesend Historical Society – Mr Benson is using his umbrella as a ranging pole!

MEMBERS OF THE GRAVESEND HISTORICAL SOCIETY posed against the wall. From the left: J. Benson, local historian who started life as 'the boy' at Paine's grocers shop (see page 74), and later had a grocers shop of his own, before becoming a journalist with Odhams Press; T.A. Reavall; A.J. Philip, first Borough Librarian and author of a history of the town; J. Horn; and the compiler of this book – the only survivor.

WAKEFIELD STREET (above) AND BATH STREET (below) built c.1830 and demolished in 1964. Now the site of the St George's Centre.

A VIEW FROM AN AEROPLANE c.1920. Top right, The World's End public house (originally the cross-ferry landing place) with Tilbury Fort. Below, with smoking chimney, Russells Brewery and cooling tower. The last local brewery was taken over by Trumans in 1931. To the left lie West Street Station Pier and goods yard and the Coal Consumers' Baltic and Fletchers wharves. One last house on Clifton Marine Parade remains next to the railway. In the foreground are the backs of the houses in Overcliffe.

CLIFTON MARINE PARADE C.1900. To the left is the new Thames Yacht Club (built in 1840 as the Clifton Hotel). The Gravesend Week in June was one of the events of the social calendar, with the Prince of Wales (later Edward VII) and his nephew, Kaiser William II, taking part in the races. The Club was wound up in 1900 and the building was a VAD hospital in the First World War, before demolition in 1937. Next along the parade the small wooden buildings were the Gravesend Bathing Station (1797), followed by the Clifton Baths, built in 1837, and Clifton Terrace with Rosherville Place and Rosherville Hotel in the distance.

THE SAME LOOKING EAST C.1890, with the West Street Station Pier in the background and Russells Brewery chimney. The whole of this area was taken over in around 1910 by Imperial Paper Mills (which closed in 1981) and is now being developed as Gravesend Industrial Estate.

LOOKING WEST FROM CLIFTON TERRACE c.1890. The Hit or Miss public house is to the left, beyond which are cottages at the end of Slaves Alley, Teapot Row, and Rosherville Place and Hotel. On the right are Fletcher's chalk and lime wharves. 'Bycliffes' lies behind the trees.

'BYCLIFFES', rear view c.1890. Home of William Fletcher, (p. 86) alderman, magistrate, church warden and entrepreneur, who, with his son and nephews, ran the chalk and lime works and imported timber and coal. Sunday School treats were held in his grounds and in 1887, when he was Mayor, he entertained the Earl of Darnley and the Council to a venison dinner. The house was demolished in 1910 (but see p. 82 for the lodge). (Gravesend Library.)

SLAVES ALLEY OR BYCLIFFES ROW C.1890 where Fletcher's chalkies and lime-burners lived. Bycliffes was over the wall behind the trees to the right. (Ford-Green Collection.)

FLETCHER'S LIME KILNS C.1890. The figures are Tom Carter, his eldest son, a boy assistant and an unidentified figure on the steps.

THE IMPERIAL PAPER MILLS. In 1909 Bycliffes Estate was sold to the Imperial Paper Mills and their new mills were built on the site. This photograph shows Clifton Marine Parade looking east around 1920, with the site of Bycliffes House and Slaves Alley to the right. (Grierson Collection.)

HIT OR MISS C.1925, surrounded by the papermills and shortly before demolition.

TEAPOT ROW 1954, just before demolition. The tenants here supplied the 'Gravesend teas' of shrimps and watercress to the trippers and visitors to Rosherville Gardens. Rosherville Place (the bay windows of one part of which can be seen) was above. Warren Hastings House now occupies this site.

ROSHERVILLE HOTEL c.1890. Built in 1835 and designed by H.E. Kendall. Visitors for the Yacht Week stayed here. It was a VAD hospital in the First World War and then became flats which were demolished in 1968. (B Hayes, from the Ford-Green Collection.)

ROSHERVILLE PIER C.1890 with one of the pleasure boats for Rosherville Gardens coming alongside. (B. Hayes, from the Ford-Green Collection.)

ROSHERVILLE GARDENS C.1890. Covering about 17 acres and opened in 1837, it was a popular place 'to spend a happy day' both for locals and Londoners. The Terrace looking east towards the Burch Road entrance.

THE TERRACE, looking west. The two men are in front of the Bear Pit. Woodfield House stands on top of the cliffs, with statues at the top of the steps which lead to the London Road entrance.

THE BIJOU THEATRE AND REFRESHMENT ROOM with the Baronial Hall in the distance. (Grierson Collection.)

THE BARONIAL HALL, used for dances, with the end of the longbar on the left. The passageway between led to the lake which was filled in in 1886/7 and thereafter used for firework displays and athletics.

THE AFRICAN BLONDIN on the tightrope. My late senior partner's brother, Ignatius Tolhurst, was said as a child to have been carried on his shoulders across the tightrope, much to the horror of his father when he found out!

A VIEW FROM THE TOWER in the previous photograph, looking across the glazed roof of the Winter Garden c.1880. The London Road Tower, built in 1864, had a clock with chimes which played tunes such as 'Oh dear, what can the matter be'. The row of elms in the background is Pelham Road.

THE TOWER c.1905. In 1900 the gardens closed and became derelict, the moveables and the clock being sold. In 1901 H.E. Porter (p. 58) and John Russell (p. 86) bought the gardens and refurbished them. This is the site of the Winter Gardens (now slot machines under an awning). The gardens were open in the summer only until 1910. Part of the site was sold to Henleys telegraph works (now GEC) in 1924 and the remainder in 1938. The tower was demolished in 1939 and the site cleared.

The Main Road

ROCHESTER ROAD c.1922 (from the Chalk Maltings cooling tower). The road was widened and improved under the Unemployment Relief Act of 1921, and all the work was done by pick and shovel to provide maximum employment. The area is now covered by Dickens Road, Bellman Avenue, etc. (Ford-Green Collection.)

DENTON COURT c.1900. Built in 1791 by Nicholas Gilbee, demolished in 1936 and Denton Court Road built on the site.

RUINS OF DENTON CHURCH c.1900. In 1901 G.M. Arnold (p. 85 & p. 86) rebuilt the church as a Roman Catholic chapel.

Denton, Gravesend.

THE GRAVESEND TRAM TERMINUS, Denton, c.1925. One of the original four-wheel cars with added top cover under way for Swanscombe. Milton Church tower and the Prince of Wales public house are also in view.

EAST MILTON ROAD c.1887. On the left is Milton Church School, built in 1859 and closed in 1938. Always known as 'The Duck Pond School' because of the pond at the rear. (It is now the parish hall.) Milton Church itself is in the centre. (Ford-Green Collection.)

PARK PLACE in 1954 shortly before demolition. Built in 1834 and designed by the architect A.H. Wilds. The building with the pediment was Queen's College, later Park House School, and after 1900 the first head office of the Associated Portland Cement Manufacturers (now Blue Circle). Finally it became the Gravesend Conservative Association HQ. It gave its name to the heavy leather gaiters worn on the cement works which were known locally as 'Park House Gaiters'.

MILTON ROAD c.1885. Left is the entrance to Harmer Street before the clock tower was built. A horse tram is at its terminus and the trees of Park Place stand in the background.

THE CLOCK TOWER was built in celebration of Queen Victoria's Golden Jubilee. The Mayor, Wm. Fletcher, laid the foundation stone on 6 September 1887. The architect was John Johnson, joint architect with Alfred Messon of the Alexandra Palace. (Ford-Green Collection.)

OPENING OF CLOCK TOWER, 5 June 1888, by the Mayor, H. Berkowitz (headmaster of the Jewish Academy, Tivoli House). A telegram was sent to Queen Victoria at Balmoral. Lord Grimthorpe, who produced the specification for Big Ben, designed the clock. Alfred Tolhurst presented the chimes. (Ford-Green Collection.)

THE CLOCK TOWER C.1900, with the four gas lamps as originally built.

PROCLAMATIONS of all sorts took place at the clock tower. This photograph shows that of King George V.

THE OLD WESLEYAN METHODIST CHURCH, built in 1812 by W. Gould and demolished in 1905. Note the advertisement for 'Pleasant Sunday Afternoons for Men and Women'. The P.S.A. Orchestra was well known locally. (Grierson Collection.)

THE NEW INN C.1890, originally the home of the Holker family. It became The New Inn in 1780 with a well-known bowling green and gardens which were built on in the 1880s. At the rear were Turners Livery and Bait Stables, the equivalent of a modern service garage. (Tilley Collection.)

TURNER'S CHARABANCS and brakes in Parrock Street, c.1900. (H.V. Spencer.)

HENRY E. PORTER rent collecting with his son, Horace A. Porter, outside his estate agents office at 182 Parrock Street c.1895. (Later Porter, Putt & Fletcher, and Porter & Cobb). (J.A. Porter.)

THE STAR PUBLIC HOUSE AND CLARENCE STREET in 1963 shortly before demolition. Now the open-air car-park. Windmill Hill is in the background.

PEPPERCROFT STREET in 1963, seen from Lord Street, and now part of the open-air car-park. It was so named after a field called 'The Peppercrofts'.

GRAVESEND FROM AN AEROPLANE. PARROCK STREET.
ROYAL TERRACE PIER. THAMES MISSION CHURCH. (A4018)

AERIAL PHOTOGRAPH, 1924, of Parrock Street and Queen Street in the centre with St John's Tower, New Inn and St Andrews. Peppercroft Street and Eden Place are to the left, with Lord Street at right angles.

KING STREET SCHOOL. Girls class at needlework in 1913. (Ford-Green Collection.)

KING STREET SCHOOL C.1880. Built in 1835, it was closed in 1928 and demolished in 1930. The site was then occupied by Barclays Bank (closed 1987) and Williamsons Cafe (now Abbey National Building Society). To the right is a cab rank. (B. Hayes, from the Ford-Green Collection.)

KING STREET C.1896, the 'new' King's Head (builder W.H. Archer), built in 1895 next to Tulks. Left is Caddells the printers, built in 1811, and right, Pinnocks Almshouses. (B. Hayes, from the Ford-Green Collection.)

PINNOCKS ALMSHOUSES c.1897. They were built in 1838 and demolished in 1898. Glover and Homewood's sale particulars are posted on the front. The County Court and Coopers furnishers shop are to the left, Windmill Street is to the right.

KING STREET c.1905. The Earl of Darnley's carriage is in the centre. The London and County Bank (now the National Westminster), built in 1898 and designed by architect Alfred Williams, and David Greigs (now a carpet shop), built in 1903 in the Arts and Crafts style, can be seen to the right where the King Street frontage of the almshouses formerly stood.

THE NELSON, built in 1806, shown here in 1875 just before demolition. Stricklands next door was destroyed in a big fire in 1887.

WINDMILL STREET c.1890. Wm. Plucks (now Bennett and Brown) has replaced Stricklands next to the 'new' Nelson of 1878 (closed 1983 and now McDonalds). Opposite is the High Street with the New Prince of Orange, built c.1805 and replaced by the Burtons building in 1928, and Bryants and Rackstraws, built c.1810 and demolished in 1957. This latter site is now occupied by Woolworths. The almshouse railings are on the right. Note the Gravesend Sanitary Laundry van. (B. Hayes, from the Ford-Green Collection.)

OPENING THE PUBLIC LIBRARY, 25 September 1905. G.M. Arnold, Mayor. Within the entrance stands A.J. Philip, the first Borough Librarian; in front of the Mayor is I.B. Berkowitz, chairman of the Library Building Committee; on the other side of the entrance Alderman J.H. Cooper, chairman of the Library Committee, H.H. Brown, Town Clerk, in a wig, with the Oar-bearer, left, and Mace-bearer, right. The library was built (architect E.J. Bennett and builder A.E. Tong) on the Windmill Street frontage where the almshouses formerly stood. The library was given by Andrew Carnegie and the site paid for by ten leading inhabitants. (Ford-Green Collection.)

NEW ROAD looking west, c.1903. The Prince of Orange, 'The Wonderful Mutoscope', Delarue and Gardens (later Bon Marche) and Prince of Orange Tap, are all in view. (Grierson Collection.)

NEW ROAD looking west, c.1912. Bon Marche has taken in 'The Wonderful Mutoscope' and is extending to the corner of Princes Street. (The hoarding is round the site of the Prince of Orange Tap). The Nelson still has only one storey at the western end. (Grierson Collection.)

NEW ROAD c.1930. Burtons has replaced the Prince of Orange. The Bon Marche is now complete (later Chiesmans and site of the present Army & Navy). Note the 'Stop me and buy one' ice-cream tricycle.

STONE STREET c.1900 (from a drawing by J.S. Kean). Steels (for three generations stonemasons) occupied the site of the present Midland Bank. Wm. R. Green's house is to the right.

STATION APPROACH from Stone Street c.1890. It is now Clive Road and the back of the Anglesea Centre. (Gravesend Library.)

MOULTON & WALLIS, STONE STREET 1892. They were a large firm of builders who later built the electricity works and tram depot, and rebuilt Swanscombe Church. The premises on the left were later Gravesend Rubber and the house (home of the Wallis family), was Martin & Son Solicitors office. The baby in the pram is the late Miss Eva Wallis.

F.A. MOORES CHEMISTS c.1903 (formerly Sharmans, then Rossiters and later Bolts), with hoardings in Princes Street.

THE SAME c.1929 surrounded by the first Marks & Spencer built in 1927 and Missings to the left, the drapers and toystore later to become British Home Stores.

NEW ROAD c.1903 with tram *en route* for Denton waiting on the passing loop. Colonial Meat Co. are on the left with their great rivals Nelson & Co., opposite, who also sold colonial meat. The first half of Missings' new building is beyond.

NEW ROAD c.1880 with Tolhurst Lovell & Clinch Solicitors office on the left. The Royal Sovereign public house is beyond with Dr Pinching's trees and the high building opposite was Boormans (now Walkers) jewellers, the first shop to have a roller blind, c.1883. The other blinds were all supported by rods in the gutter.

ALFRED TOLHURST built a new office for his firm in 1905 and a new bank 'Capital and Counties' (later Lloyds) to handle his account instead of the London County. The architect was George Clay Senior and the building was demolished in 1973 to make way for the Anglesea Centre.

ANGLESEA PLACE c.1926, at the rear of New Road. It was built by Henry Eversfield, a local auctioneer whose patron was the Marquis of Anglesea who lost a leg at Waterloo and whose name is now perpetuated in the shopping centre. (Gravesend Library.)

NEW ROAD c.1890. Mrs Missings fancy drapers with, next door, her husband's tobacconist, followed by Crofts oil and colour merchant. (B. Hayes, from the Ford-Green Collection.)

NEW ROAD C.1895. The large building to the left was E.C. Paines grocers built in 1885 by W.H. Archer. This was the first of a number of Queen Anne revival buildings in Gravesend (and the second shop to have roller blinds!). The Earl of Darnley's carriage is about to pass it. (B. Hayes, from the Ford-Green Collection.)

NEW ROAD C.1930. Paines has become Dolcis Shoes, but in spite of changes of ownership a surprising number of buildings remain from earlier views. The close-boarded fence and trees of Dr Pinching can also be seen.

75 & 76 NEW ROAD c.1954. These were built in c.1810 and demolished in 1958. For many years prior to his death in 1940, Dr C. J. Pinching occupied both houses; the right-hand one was, at one time, the home of F.B. Nettleingham, steam flour miller, councillor and JP, and later the *Gravesend Standard* was printed here. Dr Pinching was the last of three generations of Gravesend doctors, his father living at 76 New Road before him and his grandfather on The Terrace. His wife was a Miss Russell.

NEW ROAD c.1925. To the right is the Salvation Army Citadel, built in 1807 as the Theatre Royal; next is the Royal Mews, at one time William Greens, later Solomons; and finally Crescent Trading and The Eagle. Left is an electric arc lamp installed in 1903. These lamps gave a brilliant white light until the carbons burnt too far apart, when they had to be lowered by a wire controlled from a little door in the skirt and re-set.

THE SALVATION ARMY BUILDING 1969 shortly before demolition, showing its weather-board construction. Most of the older buildings in the New Road were weather-board with stucco or brick façades.

NEW ROAD C.1903, with Upton's, The Sun, Moores boot and shoe shop, Ladds greengrocers, and Merritts barbers. When my father came to Gravesend in 1905 he had his weekly bath here. No Gravesend landladies provided such a facility at the time. (Tilley Collection.)

THE UPTON FAMILY in the yard at The Sun. For over 100 years this family held the licence. Solomon Upton held the licence at the turn of the century. His widow, who succeeded him, is in the centre. Her son, Edwin, who succeeded her, is beside her, with, right, Fred Upton and Grace Upton (later Haill). The Sun was demolished in 1971.

NEW ROAD 1885. The bootblack on the right was for cleaning shoes when you reached the stones and before you went to your business premises. The large building, left, was the Public Hall built in 1880 (now Bejams). Nellie Melba, Clara Butt and her husband Kennerly Rumford, Susa's Band and Winston Churchill all appeared here. When the first regular films were shown here it was known as the Popular Picture Palace. In 1933, it was refurbished under the name of 'The Super', with a Mighty Compton organ.

ST JAMES SCHOOL C.1885, opened 1855, closed 1937. The site is now occupied by Pounces. The 'wheel' sign next door was Smiths Cycle Shop which also operated the first motor buses in 1901–1902 while the horse tramway was being electrified. (Ford-Green Collection.)

ST JAMES SCHOOL boys class 1914. (Ford-Green Collection.)

GRAVESEND MUNICIPAL TECHNICAL SCHOOL c.1895. The architect was Lt. Col. C.T. Plunkett and it was opened by Princess Beatrice on 19 July 1893. It originally incorporated an art school and the public library. It was extended in 1902, became the County School and is now the Adult Education Centre. (Ford-Green Collection.)

PRINCESS BEATRICE arriving at the Central Station with guard of honour in 1893. (Ford-Green Collection.)

BARRACK ROW c.1925. It was built in 1805 to house troops during the Napoleonic Wars. Solomons funeral cars are parked in front. Demolished c.1930. (Grierson Collection.)

THE FRUIT STALL, BARRACK ROW c.1925 (now Clive Road). (Grierson Collection.)

OVERCLIFFE, BYCLIFFE'S LODGE AND GATES 1971. In the left-hand pillar is a stone with the letters 'N.P.' marking the boundary between Gravesend and Northfleet. The backs of the houses in Pier Road are in Northfleet (for Bycliffe's House see p. 40).

SECTION THREE

The Old Road

Lion Garage – Milton Hall – Echo Square – Sun Lane – Cross Lane – Parrock Road
Windmill Hill – Singlewell Road – Houses in Old Road – Old Prince of Orange – Alms
Houses – Woodlands – Essex Road – Cemetery – Pelham Road

OLD ROAD EAST c.1921. From the south side of the Chalk Maltings cooling tower (see p. 50 for the north side). Lion Garage in the centre with the Arnold Lions (which are on the forecourt of the present garage). Arnold Transport and the Lion Garage were started by Francis ('Fingey') Arnold, a grandson of G.M. Arnold. (Ford-Green Collection.)

MILTON HALL, The gates and drive (now Pine Avenue) c.1900. The lions on the pillars are now in the garden of the left-hand lodge which, much extended, still survives.

MILTON HALL entrance c.1900. Built in 1873 and demolished in 1930, this was the largest private house in the old Borough. It was the home of George Matthews Arnold, London solicitor and Roman Catholic convert. He was eight times Mayor, although not a member of the corporate body, and brother of Sir Edwin Arnold, the poet and orientalist, Sir R.A. Arnold MP and A.A. Arnold, the Rochester solicitor. His grandfather and great-grandfather were Mayors and bakers in West Street. They made their money supplying ships' biscuits. (Gravesend Historical Society Collection.)

MILTON HALL garden side c.1900 (architect, Somers-Clark). G.M. Arnold was succeeded by his son, Bernard (also a solicitor), in 1908 and on his death in 1924 the estate was sold for building land. (Gravesend Historical Society Collection.)

MILTON HALL from Church Walk. The hall and entrance are in the centre with pine trees to the right. (Gravesend Historical Society Collection.)

G.M. ARNOLD'S GOLDEN WEDDING 1893. Front row, left to right: G. Butchard, engineer (p. 10); J. Hanks Cooper, house furnisher (p. 111); G. Wood, brewer (p. 110 & p. 22); Mrs E.C. Arnold; G.M. Arnold; J. Russell, brewer, who at one time lived at Glenthorne (p. 100), later Hillside (and was charged with electricity by F.J. Ebdon, a medical electrician in Darnley Street, on his way to work each morning); W. Fletcher, lime and timber merchant (p. 40); finally, this looks like E.C. Paine, grocer (p. 74 & p. 104), but it ought to be J.G.L. Tulk, outfitter (p. 62), the remaining Alderman. Behind G. Wood stands A. Tolhurst, solicitor. Behind Mr Arnold are, to the left, W.J. King, Borough Treasurer, and right, E.E. Hatton, Town Clerk. (Gravesend Historical Society Collection.)

THE MARKET COLUMNS c.1900. G.M. Arnold was a keen local historian with an extensive museum in the grounds of Milton Hall. In 1898 when the present market hall was erected the Council presented him with the columns from Fowler's 1818 market. They still survive in the back garden of 30 Pine Avenue. (Gravesend Historical Society Collection.)

OLD ROAD EAST c.1900. The chimneys on the right belong to Milton Grange (formerly Ivy Cottage). Opposite is the entrance to Milton Hall, with the gate to the left being the entrance to Parrock Hall.

OLD ROAD EAST c.1905. The house to the left, built in 1904, was known as 'Passingworth', later 'Greyfriars' and now serves as an old people's home. The cows probably belonged to Dr Skipworth, a keen agriculturalist who later farmed in Ireland.

PARROCK HALL c.1905. Built in 1761 by Peter Moulson, in the latter half of the nineteenth century it was a boys' home run in conjunction with The Little Boys Homes at Farningham. In 1905 it was occupied by George Sharland, Clerk of the Peace. In 1928 it was converted into flats and still survives in Joy Road. (Tilley Collection.)

FOUNTAIN AND OLD ROAD, GRAVESEND.

ECHO SQUARE C.1905. The public house was built in 1865 and named after a famous echo which could be heard in the valley where Parrock Avenue is now. The drinking fountain was erected in 1903 in memory of Kendrick and Annie Martha Gibbons. Note Johnson's horse-drawn tank wagon which delivered paraffin.

A HERD OF SHEEP being driven across Echo Square C.1932. (Ford-Green Collection.)

THE WEST KENT HUNT meeting at Echo Square c.1905. Parrock Farm is in the background.

PARROCK FARM c.1900. Built 1620–30 as a timber-frame house with butt-side purlins; a Georgian front was added c.1775. Charles Smart (after whom Smarts Road is named) was the tenant-farmer between 1862 and 1886. In 1907 the house was bought by John Russell jun. who lived there until 1934.

THE OLD SUN COTTAGE c.1908 shortly before demolition. At one time it was a beerhouse (it had lost its licence by 1797), and was mentioned in 1665 when 'a nurse' and 'a maid' at *Ye Sun* were buried at Milton. (Ford-Green Collection.)

SUN LANE c.1910. Note the board of the Gravesend Land Co. advertising building plots on Parrock Farm land. (Tilley Collection.)

SUN POND in flood c.1900. The late Mr A. Lintott and a friend paddling. The pond was opposite the end of Portland Avenue. (Ford-Green Collection.)

CROSS LANE c.1905. The Whitehill Road post office was opened in 1899. Mrs Hopper was postmistress and later her daughter. It closed in 1982. There was a well-known rookery in the elms beyond until c.1925 and an annual rook shoot was held at Echo Square. (Tilley Collection.)

MILTON MOUNT COLLEGE c.1900. This was built in 1873 as a school for the daughters of nonconformist ministers, but later opened to others. The school moved to Cirencester in 1915 due to the Zeppelin raids. The building was then taken over by the Admiralty who used it as a hospital for VD cases. When they found out, the school refused to return. It became a Roman Catholic orphanage run by Southwark Rescue and, after serving as the WVS HQ during the Second World War, it was demolished in 1972.

MILTON MOUNT – THE STUDIO. The first headmistress was Miss Selina Hadland (1873–89) who was associated with Miss Buss and Miss Beale (of the Cheltenham Ladies College) as pioneers of ladies' education. It was the first school in the country to teach domestic science. (Larkin Collection.)

MILTON MOUNT c.1905. Fire drill. My mother-in-law, who attended the school as a day girl in the 1900s, well remembers using these 'shoots'. (Tilley Collection.)

MILTON MOUNT. Girls playing hockey on G.M. Arnold's meadow at Milton Hall c.1905, now the site of the Boys' Grammar School. (Gravesend Historical Society Collection.)

PARROCK ROAD c.1905, before the second carriageway was built.

WINDMILL HILL from Friston's print c.1850 with the bank holiday crowds which thronged the hill and patronised the Bell Vue Hotel, the camera obscura and the look-out platform built round the mill.

WINDMILL HILL c.1890. The holiday crowds have departed. Melbourne Villa on the left is derelict. The observatory, whose camera obscura was a rival to the mill's, is boarded up and a high fence erected round The Bell Vue. (Tilley Collection.)

BAYNARD CASTLE. Sheppy Place, built c.1846 by Edward Lacey (Mayor in 1850), a local builder who went bankrupt. It was used as a high school by Milton Mount College, later becoming Gutteridges Girls School, and the Misses Shewsburys. It was demolished in 1952. The site is now part of Wrotham Road School. (Tilley Collection.)

THE MILL shortly before its demolition in 1894.

THE BELL VUE closed in 1897 and the Corporation bought the top of the hill from John Russell.

THE RUINS OF THE BELL VUE in 1900 after the 'bloods' of the town had set it alight on Mafeking Night and cut the fire brigade's hoses to prevent them putting it out.

SINGLEWELL ROAD c.1880 from a point near the present Central Parade. The first cross hedge is now Cross Lane. The second to the left is Old Road West. The Prince of Orange is behind the trees with West Hill House above and Windmill Hill, Kings Cottages, Constitution Crescent and the Waterworks chimney (demolished in 1973) on the skyline. The houses in Old Road East from the right are: Glenthorne, demolished in 1971, Torquay Villas (at No. 1 lived Frederick Leith, a builder and Mayor in 1867) which survive, Dunton House, demolished in 1971 (see p. 104), Amoy Cottage, Rose Villa (see p. 105) and Lorraine.

SINGLEWELL ROAD c.1910. The houses to the left were built in the 1880s by H.W. and J.G. Martin, those on the right in 1906 by P. Martin. They had electric light laid on. When my grandfather bought No. 20 new he was so uncertain about electricity that he had gas lights installed as well! Badman's Cemetery Nurseries to the right, the last part of which survived until c.1950. Also visible are the railings of the Singlewell Road Chapel.

SINGLEWELL FIELDS c.1914, now Central Avenue, from a point near the present Central Hotel. Left is St Faith's Church, built in 1906 and demolished in 1976, with the backs of houses in Cross Lane, built 1912/13, to the right.

SINGLEWELL FIELDS C.1900. There are no houses in Cross Lane except Elnatham Cottages, built in 1886. To the right is Dalton's smallholding, to the left, Milton Court and above is Milton Mount. (Grierson Collection.)

MILTON COURT built c.1865 for William Simpson after he moved from Chiltern Lodge due to the invasion of his privacy by Rosherville Gardens Tower. For many years it was the residence of George Lucas JP, a local dentist.

MILTON COURT entrance, demolished in 1974. The architects were Strong & Parr, and a curious type of hexagonal brick filled with granite chippings was used. A small section of the wall and the coach house in Spring Grove survive.

GEORGE DANIEL HUMPHREYS, Channel Trinity House pilot and his wife, Catherine Hannah, with some of their sixteen children, eight boys and eight girls. The last two of each were given the second Christian names of Septimus and Octavious (boys) and Septima and Octavia (girls). My father-in-law, centre, who was the seventh son, was always called 'Sep'. The six sons who grew up all went to sea, three becoming Trinity House pilots. They lived at 'Glenthorne' (p. 100) which had an extensive garden between Old Road and Cross Lane (with a tunnel under the road), on which they later built a new house called 'Glendillon' (later the United Reform Church).

MRS E.C. PAINE. Dunton House also had a garden on the opposite side of Old Road and was the residence of Alderman E.C. Paine (see p. 74 & p. 86). Mrs Paine was formerly a Mrs Anthony and at one time matron of Milton Mount.

AMOY COTTAGE c.1880, with the stables of Rose Villa to the left and the waterworks chimney. The cottage was built in 1854 by W. Gould for William Zabell, a master mariner. It also had a garden on the south side of the road. Dunton House is to the right.

ROSE VILLA C.1922. Built in 1854, it became the original Convent High School of 1922 which moved to 'Glenthorne' in 1928.

OLD PRINCE OF ORANGE c.1925 with one of the small 'direct-stair' trams at the terminus. Note also the milk float with a churn from which milk was delivered by scoop into a jug or can, and the Hillman(?) car with a spare petrol can on the running board.

OLD PRINCE OF ORANGE in 1931 just before demolition. 'Trumans Beers' have replaced 'Russell's Shrimp Brand Beers'. The traffic-lights were the first in the town with a 40-second fixed interval.

OLD ROAD WEST c.1905. The gates on the right lead to 'Elmfield' built in 1902 for W. Fletcher (see p. 40 & p. 86). It is now a doctors' and dentists' surgery with flats. (Grierson Collection.)

THE 'NEW' PINNOCKS' ALMSHOUSES c.1905, built in 1897 to replace the King Street ones (p. 64) and designed by architects F.R. Farrow and B.C.H. Nisbett. Mrs E.C. Arnold (p. 86) laid the foundation stone of the common room on 15 September 1898. The first block next to the common room has been demolished (1988) due to subsidence. (Grierson Collection.)

REEDS COTTAGES c.1897. These belonged to the parish and were used by the Cholera Morbis Committee in 1832 for housing cholera victims, and by the parish for housing the poor. The site was bought by Pinnocks Charity in 1897 for the 'new' almshouses.

EVES NURSERY (formerly Clarke's), Wrotham Road c.1885, occupied a site south of the Bat & Ball in the area now covered by Essex Road and Kent Road. (Gravesend Library.)

A WALK IN EVES NURSERY C.1885. (Gravesend Library.)

THE BANDSTAND, EVES NURSERY. The nursery was expanded to cater for visitors to the town and included the Pavilion Theatre. (Gravesend Library.)

ESSEX ROAD c.1905. The last of the nurseries (then Coombes) are to the right.

WOODLANDS c.1910. The house was built in 1893 for George Wood the brewer (see p. 86 and p. 22) who had bought the site and the adjoining meadow in 1884 from his brother, John Wood, of Craggs Farm and Westfield Singlewell, farmer and brickmaker. It became a hotel (now a Berni Inn) in 1934. (Tilley Collection.)

DASHWOOD HOUSE built c.1820 (later extended ?). It was the home of John Hanks Cooper (p. 86), the house furnisher and later of C. Percy Taylor, Chief Engineer APCM, who married Miss Wood, the brewer's daughter from Woodlands. The house was demolished in 1971.

THE VICTORIA GARDENS, Old Road West, opened in 1834. In 1839 they were sold to the Gravesend and Milton Cemetery Co. The dance hall and tea room is the present cemetery chapel.

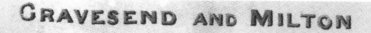

GRAVESEND AND MILTON

CEMETERY

INCORPORATED BY ACT OF PARLIAM 1ST VICT

1838

ENTRANCE LODGE

Stephen Geary

CEMETERY GATES – the architect's drawing for the cemetery gates in 1838. They were built in 1840 and recently restored by the Corporation. Stephen Geary, who designed the gates and laid out the cemetery, was the architect for Highgate and a number of other well-known cemeteries. (Gravesend Historical Society Collection.)

PELHAM ROAD c.1887. On the right can be seen the White Post, built in 1844, and Wolseley Terrace, built 1885. The roofs of the houses on the south side of Old Road can be seen. The cows belong to Wm. Cackett of Manor Farm. This field is now the Girls Grammar School with houses on the road frontages. (B. Hayes, from the Ford-Green Collection.) (For another view of Pelham Road see p. 155.)

I.C. JOHNSON'S 100th birthday, 28 January 1911. He claimed to be the inventor of Portland Cement in 1844 (although Aspdin seems to have been first). As manager of White's Works, Swanscombe, he appreciated the importance of chemical control. His house, Mayfield in Pelham Road, was built in 1875 of concrete. A presentation by his fellow cement manufacturers at the time is shown. Standing are F.A. White (Swanscombe), E. Charleton (Johnson & Partners), J.F. Spoor (his partner at Gateshead), and H. Earl (Hull). Sitting: A. Tolhurst (Red Lion, Northfleet), C.H. Watson (Greenhithe), I.C. Johnson, C. Charleton (Johnson's sales director), F. Bazeley White (Swanscombe, MP for Gravesend 1885–92).

Watling Street

Cobham Woods – Valley Drive – King's Farm – Singlewell – Tollgate – Hog Lane

WATLING STREET, Cobham Woods c.1900.

WATLING STREET, Cobham Woods c.1922, during the construction of the new arterial road. (Gravesend Library.)

CHARCOAL BURNING, Cobham Woods, Battle Street c.1920.

WHITEHILL LANE c.1900, now Valley Drive, near the junction with Dobson Road.

Kings Farm Estate, Gravesend.

KINGS FARM ESTATE c.1923 – Gravesend's first council estate. The Mayor, W.J. Harrington (p. 126), cut the first sod on 6 January 1921. George and Neville King were the farmers who gave their name to 'King's Farm'. They and Mr Christian (who had a cottage in Whitehill Lane) supplied stones from their fields to the Vestries for roadmaking. (Larkin Collection.)

THE GEORGE, SINGLEWELL c.1900. The licensee was F.S. Jackson.

SINGLEWELL 1881. To the left are Corner Cottages and the well; to the right Hever Court, built 1675 and demolished 1952. Hever Court was the manor house of Ifield and its predecessor was the original home of the Hevers.

HEVER COURT 1881. The garden with Orchard Farm (which survives) to the right.

THE WELL AT SINGLEWELL c.1895. Right is Ifield House occupied by H.W. Martin, wheelwright, engineer and parish clerk. The site of his workshop at the rear is now a garage and petrol station. Left is the Chapel Farm residence of Wm. Bliss, farmer and Ifield church warden.

THE REAR WALL OF CHAPEL FARM 1956, which incorporates the remains of the medieval chapel at Singlewell.

CRAGGS FARM barn and cottages in 1956, demolished c.1958. When threshing, a traction engine was placed on the grass outside the midstrey to provide motive power. Now Hever Court Road.

TOLLGATE INN, Northumberland Bottom c.1920, from Watling Street.

TOLLGATE INN c.1890, from Wrotham Road looking towards Meopham. The left-hand cottage is the old tollgate keeper's cottage for the Wrotham turnpike. When the Turnpike Trust was wound up in 1876, the cottage was occupied by a boot repairer named Richardson who had collected the tolls and so continued in 1886. It was demolished c.1900.

THE VIADUCT c.1922. Tipping chalk for the new Watling Street. The inn was eventually buried beneath the embankment and the new road was opened by the Prince of Wales (later the Duke of Windsor) on 19 November 1924.

WATLING STREET c.1922, from a point near Coldharbour Road. Tip trucks to the left show work has started on the new road. Wrotham Road and the Tollgate Inn and Farm are in the middle distance and the elms on the skyline at the entrance to Ifield Court Road. Exeter House is near the top of the hill to the left.

WATLING STREET in 1963; the same view just before the road was 'motorised' and the dual carriageway built (opened in August 1966). The same elms can be seen on the skyline. The 1924 Tollgate Inn is on the right in the middle distance.

NORTHUMBERLAND BOTTOM FARM 1963. These were the only buildings left when the 1924 road was built (it can be seen above on the embankment). They were buried by the 1966 road and are the site of the Turnpike Garage and roundabout.

THE JUNCTION OF HOGG LANE (opposite) with Watling Street and Downs Road, c.1905. Standing is Dr R. Austin-Freeman, author of the Dr Thorndyke detective stories. The chalk hole in which the body was found in 'The Green Check Jacket' was in the middle of the field behind the trees to the left.

BEATING THE NEW BOROUGH BOUNDS 1935. The party in front of the Tollgate Hotel are from the left: Sergeant-at-mace J. Parkinson; -?-; F.T. Grant, Borough Surveyor; Cllr. N. Cooper (grandson of J. Hanks Cooper p. 86), house furnisher; Cllr. A.G. Ramsay, postman; -?-; Alderman J. Berry (wearing glasses), china & glass merchant; behind him is Cllr. A.W. Howcroft of the waterworks. Front: Cllr. G.A. Pratt, house furnisher; Cllr. J. Everden, retired grocer (light trilby); Alderman W.E. Thomas, builder; H. Gooding, builder; Alderman H. Huggins, (raising his bowler), with G.A. Penman, Borough Coroner, behind; Cllr. G.E. Morris, licensee of the Old Prince of Orange; Cllr. W.H.B. McKenzie, first Labour Mayor; Revd H.J. Powell, rector of Milton; H.H. Brown, Town Clerk; Alderman J.A. Axcell, mineral water manufacturer; Cllr. J.W. Clunn; Cllr. G.R. Croft, Co-op manager; Alderman J.W. Harrington (at rear with glasses); Cllr. Hagard, doctor; Cllr. W.L. Simmonds; Gardener who was assistant Town Clerk (with dark hair at the rear); Cllr. R.T. Lester (with bowler); -?-; J.E. Baker, sanitary inspector; Harold Tuffee, Clerk of the Peace (at the rear, with one eye); H.H. Bennett (wearing plus fours).

THE SAME PARTY ON THE MARSHES; boys with their wands, and F.T. Grant, H.H. Bennett and Gardiner. Note the new boundary stone behind the fence.

HOPPING AT SOUTHFLEET 1903, with vines grown up poles instead of wiring and stringing.

The Churches

St George's Gravesend – S.S. Peter & Paul Milton – St John's – Holy Trinity – St James – Christchurch – St Margaret, Ifield.

THE PARISH CHURCH OF GRAVESEND. St George's south side, c.1965. Its architect Charles Sloane was a local man, and it was built in 1732 with a grant from the coal dues under the '50 Churches Act' of Queen Anne, to replace an earlier church burnt down in the great fire of 1727.

St. George's Parish Church of Gravesend (Exterior).

ST GEORGE, north-west side, c.1920, showing the tower and aisle by W. & C.A. Basset-Smith.

ST GEORGE, INTERIOR c.1890, decorated for harvest festival. To the left is the original north gallery, and to the right the south gallery of 1818, both demolished in 1897. The apse was rebuilt as a chancel in 1892. The open sittings had replaced box pews in 1872 and were replaced by chairs in 1970. The glass in the east window was given by Col. W.T. Gladdish (of Bycliffes p. 40) in 1866 in memory of his wife.

LAYING THE FOUNDATION STONE for the north aisle by the Bishop of Rochester, E.S. Talbot, on 3 August 1897. The stone was presented by the Freemasons. Mr Charles Bassett-Smith, the architect, presented a silver trowel and Mr and Mrs W. Fletcher held a garden party at Bycliffes (p. 40) for a large number of friends to meet the Bishop and Mrs Talbot. Sir Gilbert Parker MP is to the left of the stone with the Bishop, Wm Fletcher, church warden, behind him and the Rector Revd J.H. Haslam on the right.

INTERIOR OF ST GEORGE'S c.1925. The small altar in the north aisle was given in 1921 in memory of Charles Adelbert Walkey, a chorister killed in action in 1915. The fine Clayton and Bell reredos in the chancel was part of the 1892 work, but it was discarded in 1970, as were the angels in the roof painted from lantern slides by the Revd Haslam.

POCAHONTAS WINDOWS. In 1914 the Colonial Dames of America in the state of Virginia cut the two east nave windows and filled them with stained glass by Powell & Son in memory of Pocahontas. This photograph shows the dedication by the Bishop of Rochester in the presence of the American ambassador on the 16 July 1914. The windows had just been unveiled and the American flag can be seen on the right.

THE BONES. In 1923 a committee was set up to find the bones of Pocahontas. Mr J. Page Gaston, an American, obtained an order for exhumation from the Home Office to open the deep brick vault of a local brickmaker Mr Curd, who had died in 1822 and into whose grave all the skulls and bones found in the 1892 and 1897 extensions had been thrown. In this view can be seen Canon Gedge, J. Everden, church warden, and Mr W.P. Pycroft round the Curd grave.

Some 78 skulls were found. Mr W.P. Pycroft, the well-known anthropologist from the British Museum, is measuring the skulls. This desecration of the churchyard caused a local outcry, but no evidence of Pocahontas was found.

ST GEORGE'S CHOIR OUTING C.1926. A Maidstone & District Tilling-Stevens electro-petrol charabanc. Back row, from left: J. Berry, – ? –, – ? –, William H. Hammond, F. Tunbridge, Revd Elliott, Mitchell (rector), H.A. Colyer, Wilfred R. Hammond. Among the ladies were Mrs E. Everden, centre, with, to her left, Mrs W.A. Hammond and to her right Mrs C.M. Moss. In the centre of the row of boys is H. Moss.

Gravesend Parish Church
St. George's.

PRESENTED TO *HOWARD MOSS ESQ* AS A SMALL MEMENTO OF
THE AFFECTION AND ESTEEM OF THE MEMBERS OF
ST GEORGE'S CHOIR DURING THE 40 YEARS OF HIS VALUED
SERVICE AS ORGANIST AND CHOIRMASTER
OCT 18TH 1931

ST GEORGE'S CHOIR. Howard Moss was the last of a Gravesend family of five, all of whom were professional musicians and teachers of music. The church wardens are F.T. Grant and J. Everden. The back row includes: H.A. Colyer, W.R. Hammond and F. Tunbridge; and the second row: E. Hadlow, Tidmarsh, H. Moss, Revd H.T. Southgate, rector, Mrs C.M. Moss, W.A. Hammond, J. Law, J. Upton, G. Parsons (as a boy, now a retired bank manager). Boys in front of the rector include G. Haill, J.A. Sparrow, (now a retired builders' merchant), -?-, G. Hall (fair hair, killed in RAF), David Sparrow (killed when an RAF night fighter pilot; the rector's stall is in his memory): at the end of the row is J. Tatchell (retired, ICI).

REVD J.H. HASLAM, rector 1892–99. He built the chancel and new vestries in 1892, the north aisle in 1897 and then removed the north and south galleries. He provided a permanent cross and candles on a gradine or rear table, painted angels in the apse and a Nativity, Crucifixion, and Moses and the Brazen Serpent. Two of his friends gave the Clayton and Bell reredos. All these improvements have gone. He also had the south windows filled with stained glass. The pulpit is his memorial.

REVD E.L. GEDGE, rector 1899–1925. He went blind on his honeymoon before he came to Gravesend, but was a popular preacher and the last one to fill the church to capacity with chairs up the gangways at festivals and evensong. The extension of the wood panelling in the chancel is his memorial.

THE PARISH CHURCH OF MILTON, SS Peter and Paul, c.1890. Basically a single cell church of the early fourteenth century with no chancel (the absence of which has recently been confirmed by an excavation of the Gravesend Historical Society). In 1790 after some lead had been stolen, the roof was removed, the walls heightened some two feet and an all-over drip-eves roof of slate put on by Thos. Hall of Dartford. The church was re-opened in 1792.

MILTON CHURCH, INTERIOR, c.1900. The 'Strawberry Hill' Gothic reredos of 1819 (cost £89 8s.) contrasts strangely with the altar rails and 'correct' Gothic of the pulpit designed by R.C. Carpenter in 1852. The north gallery also dates from 1819. Like St George's, Milton also installed a gradine for the cross and candlesticks which survived until 1988, the last in the town. The glass in the east window was given in 1852 as a memorial to the first Dr Pinching (see p. 74). The outer panels were blown out by a bomb which fell in Raphael Road on 2 September 1940. The centre panel of the 'Risen Lord' remains, the only stained glass in the church. The 'drawing room' ceiling dates from 1792.

REPLACING THE VANE ON MILTON CHURCH February 1955. W.G. Harpum (p. 21), who was for many years church warden at Milton and who was responsible for the decorative sconces and iron work in the church, carried out this work. The previous vane was dated 1842 and the Crown and Prince of Wales feathers are said to commemorate the pealing of bells when Queen Victoria and the infant Prince of Wales passed the church in 1842. The vane was damaged in a storm in 1986 and sadly when it was repaired the Prince of Wales feathers were omitted.

Roman Catholic Church, Gravesend *yours as ever Lucretie*,

ST JOHN THE EVANGELIST, Gravesend, c.1900. The first attempt to provide additional church accommodation in Gravesend was a proprietory chapel built in 1834. The architect was William Jenkins of Red Lion Square. Problems arose and it was sold to the Roman Catholic Church in 1851. The tower was added by Goldie and Child in 1873 and a convent school built, run by the Sisters of Mercy, who were also responsible for the schools in Old Road East (Larkin Collection.)

HOLY TRINITY CHURCH 1962, before demolition in 1963. Built in 1844 by architect J. Wilson, it was at one time the 'fashionable' church in the town, supported by the pilots and the waterside fraternity. Here was held from 1908 the annual Pilot's Service on Trinity Sunday which some of the elder brethren of Trinity House attend (now moved to St George's).

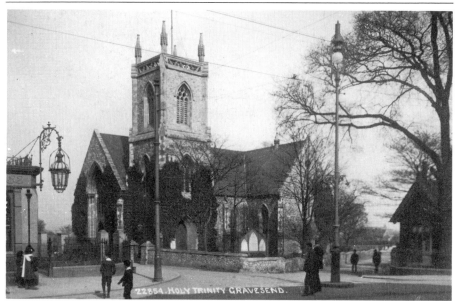

TRINITY CHURCH from the south west c.1905, with the corner of 'The Globe' public house visible to the left. It is said that when Charles R. Green was organist (a position he held for 44 years prior to his death in 1915) he always had a pint of beer waiting for him at The Globe during the sermon, there being a convenient door in the north transept, under the very fine organ, through which he could escape. A practice followed by his successor, J.E. Pressley, who was headmaster of Trinity School. The story is of course told of the vicar who preached a short sermon and had no music for the last hymn! (Grierson Collection.)

TRINITY CHURCH, INTERIOR, c.1910. The organ is in the gallery to the left. The chapel under the north gallery was furnished in memory of G.D. and C.H. Humphreys (p. 103), that under the south gallery in memory of A.G.W. Carter.

DEMOLITION OF TRINITY CHURCH, 1963.

ST JAMES CHURCH c.1890. Built in 1852 and designed by architect S.W. Dawkes, it was said to have been modelled on Poynings, Sussex. It was demolished in 1968. Note the horse trough installed in 1887 (see also p. 150). (B. Hayes, from the Ford-Green Collection.)

ST JAMES, INTERIOR, c.1890; probably the original arrangements.

ST JAMES, INTERIOR, c.1920, with the new reredos showing the Last Supper given in memory of G.L. Couchman in 1902. It was replaced by an oak table (now at Cobham) in 1952, when St James replaced St George's as the parish church of Gravesend. In 1968 St George's became the parish church once more.

CHRIST CHURCH C.1905. It was built in 1856 by architect R.C. Carpenter and, after his death, W. Slater. It was probably the most satisfying architecturally of the three Victorian Gothic churches. Unfortunately the intended spire was never built.

CHRIST CHURCH, INTERIOR, c.1905. Note the fine 'fishnet' east window and well-moulded arcades.

CHRIST CHURCH DEMOLITION. In 1932 Christ Church became unsafe and was demolished, but it was re-erected on a new site in Old Road East near Echo Square.

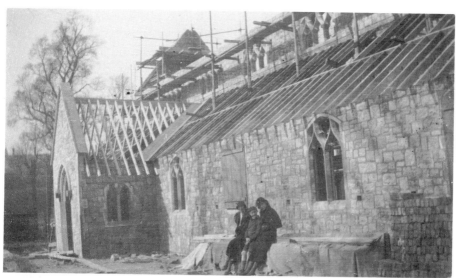

THE NEW CHRIST CHURCH. Re-building in Old Road East in 1936, looking west, the new entrance being on the south side. The foundation stone was laid on the 16 October 1934 by Florence, countess of Darnley. The Darnley family had been active on the original building committee in 1856.

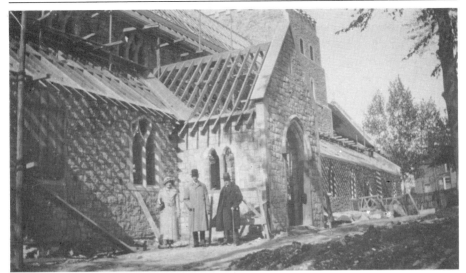

THE SAME, looking east. The architect was George E. Clay and a clerestory and 'open roof' were provided which has made the church much lighter.

THE PARISH CHURCH OF IFIELD. St Margaret c.1900. The whole church has been covered with roughcast for many years, the only medieval feature being a 'low side' window visible in the roughcast. From the measurements however it would appear to be a simple two-cell Norman fabric of which there are a number in the area.

IFIELD CHURCH, INTERIOR, c.1890, decorated for harvest festival. All the window tracery was inserted in 1845 in perpendicular form, but with 'deep external splays of pre-archaeological gothic' (Newman). The stained glass in the east window is in memory of Charles Beckett, aged 10, son of Charles Andrew Beckett the Gravesend brewer (p. 18) who lived at Hever Court (p. 119). There are a number of other windows in memory of members of the Beckett family.

SECTION SIX

Local Transport

Railways - Tramways - Omnibuses

ACCIDENT at Gravesend Central in 1893 which demolished the down-side signal box. (Pickering, Ford-Green Collection.)

CENTRAL STATION looking east c.1905. The only known photograph (there is an early line drawing) showing the awnings covering the platform lines. This was the standard SER practice for larger stations. Note the sheep in open trucks. In 1905 the RSPCA prosecuted a porter and foreman for cruelty to 96 sheep packed in two trucks; five were found dead.

CENTRAL STATION looking west c.1910, after the 'over-line' awnings were replaced by platform awnings. The buildings are the original ones of 1849 by Samuel Beazley, who was the architect of the stations on the North Kent line (for an exterior view see p. 80).

CENTRAL STATION looking east c.1920. The down-side signal box was at the end of the down platform. The station is a scheduled building and has recently been restored.

A VIEW FROM THE STATION CAR-PARK 1965, showing the water tank and lamp room, left, with the old stables on the right. St James Church is visible just before demolition and the former County School with the 1902 extension now the Victoria Building (see p. 79).

WEST STREET STATION 1923, built in 1886 by the London Chatham & Dover Railway, the South Eastern's great rival. The line, left, led to the pier and was used at one time for a service to Clacton. From 1916–1939 it was used by the Batavier Boats for their service to Holland and the line had a boat-train. The ordinary service was always meagre, five trains per day except on Saturday afternoons.

WEST STREET STATION 1953. The Saturday afternoon 'push and pull' at the town platform and the goods yard. Passenger operation ceased on 1 August 1953 and goods in 1968, and the line and station have now been completely dismantled.

DENTON CROSSING c.1900. A halt was built here in 1906 and continued until the Allhallows service was withdrawn in 1961.

ONE-HORSE TRAM C.1890. A 3ft. 6in. gauge tramway was built from Gravesend to Northfleet in 1883. It owned four cars like this and an open-sided 'toast-rack' car for the Rosherville Gardens trippers in the summer. The horse had a small bell which 'tinkled mournfully' as it went along.

TWO-HORSE TRAM. In 1898 four open-topped cars were obtained. G.H. Brooke of West Court Chalk supplied the horses, which were also used for the dustcarts and fire engine. When a fire occurred the market bell was rung and the horses removed from the nearest tram to pull the engine. (Tilley Collection.)

A TWO-HORSE BUS which belonged to the Tramway Company at Huggens College, Northfleet. Note the advertising space 'to let' on the top deck.

LAYING THE ELECTRIC TRAMWAY 1901/2. The gang with foreman and engineer, and the chimneys of two tar-burners at Clarence Place loop Windmill Street. The Gravesend and Northfleet Electric Tramways were a subsidiary of The British Electric Traction Co. and they rebuilt the line to standard gauge, extending to Denton and Swanscombe with a branch along Windmill Street and a loop via Pelham Road, Old Road West and Dover Road to Northfleet. (Though they always operated as two branches.)

AN EIGHT-WHEEL CAR working the shuttle service between St James's Church and Pelham Arms c.1903. The original fleet (of twenty) had ten of these cars seating 67 passengers. They were far too big for Gravesend and were all sold to other BET companies by 1906, being replaced by six small four-wheelers. Note the water cart laying the dust. (Gravesend Library Collections.)

DEMI-CAR AT PRINCE OF ORANGE c.1904. Two of these small one-man cars were bought for the Windmill Street and Dover Road services in 1904. They were fitted with John Raworth's regenerative equipment which fed current back into the wires when coasting downhill. The fare was reduced to $\frac{1}{2}d$. When this was put up to $\frac{3}{4}d$. c.1911 the driver was issued with packets of pins for change. (See p. 106 for a later view of The Prince of Orange terminus.) (Larkin Collection.)

THE SHRIMP BRAND TRAM c.1904. Russell's Gravesend Brewery always used one of the small open-top trams to advertise Shrimp Brand beers. This is a view at the George and Dragon, Swanscombe, the normal western terminus. The intended link with the Dartford system at Horns Cross was never built due to opposition from the SER.

THREE OF THE ORIGINAL FOUR-WHEEL CARS lying derelict (for sale £5 open-top and £10 closed) at Dover Road depot after the system closed on 28 February 1929. Beadle Bros. of Dartford put closed tops on some of the original cars c.1923. This was taken with the first film of my No. 2 Brownie camera!

A BURFORD SINGLE DECKER. In 1913 the tramway company built a bus depot in Dover Road and started to operate motor buses to Dartford and Chatham.

AN OPEN-TOP DAIMLER at Dartford c.1914. The fleet name was then 'Gravesend', later 'North Kent'.

THE MAIDSTONE AND DISTRICT BUS DEPOT c.1923. They took over the tramway bus services in 1920 and built their own depot and office on Overcliffe at the corner of Stuart Road (now a DIY store). (Ford-Green Collection.)

THE GRAVESEND AND DISTRICT CO.'S BUSES c.1927. From the left: a Karrier, three Morris Commercials (the centre one was always known as 'the coffin'), the second Karrier, and an International (there was a second one not in view). The drivers from the left were: Hugh Hind, Arthur Simmons, Albert Cousins, Fred West, Albert Hind, Harry ?, Harry Bentley, Albert Simmons. This company pioneered The Clock Tower, Darnley Road, Perry Street, Waterdales and the Wrotham Road, Cross Lane, Singlewell Road, King's Farm routes and played a large part in the demise of the trams. The Karriers worked the Perry Street route, the Internationals, Singlewell Road. They later had a number of 20-seater Dennis buses. (A. Simmonds.)